The Job of a CIVIC LEADER

Governor

Stephanie Gaston

I0800387

Table of Contents

A Starfish Book

SEAHORSE PUBLISHING

Teaching Tips for Caregivers:

As a caregiver, you can help your child succeed in school by giving them a strong foundation in language and literacy skills and a desire to learn to read.

This book helps children grow by letting them practice reading skills.

Reading for pleasure and interest will help your child to develop reading skills and will give your child the opportunity to practice these skills in meaningful ways.

- Encourage your child to read on her own at home
- Encourage your child to practice reading aloud
- Encourage activities that require reading
- Establish a reading time
- Talk with your child
- Give your child writing materials

Teaching Tips for Teachers:

Research shows that one of the best ways for students to learn a new topic is to read about it.

Before Reading

- Read the "Words to Know" and discuss the meaning of each word.
- Read the back cover to see what the book is about.

During Reading

- When a student gets to a word that is unknown, ask them to look at the rest of the sentence to find clues to help with the meaning of the unknown word.
- Ask the student to write down any pages of the book that were confusing to them.

After Reading

- Discuss the main idea of the book.
- Ask students to give one detail that they learned in the book by showing a text dependent answer from the book.

Governor

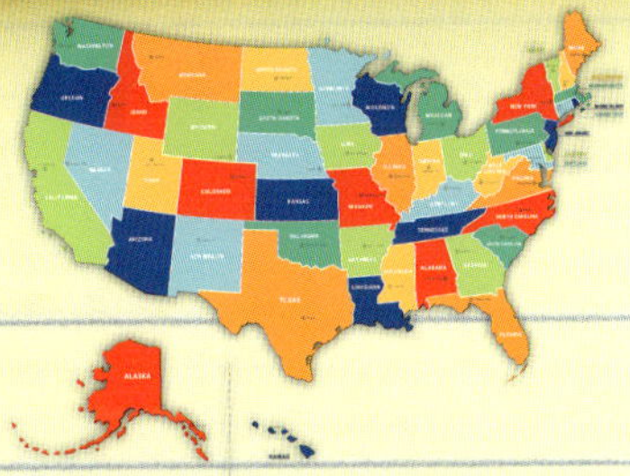

A Governor leads the **government** of a state.

There are 50 Governors in the United States.

States have different rules
about who can be Governor.

Some rules say the Governor must be older than a certain age.

Some rules say the Governor must be a U.S. **citizen**.

The people of each state vote for their Governor.

In 48 states, the Governor is elected for a **term** of four years.

In Vermont and New Hampshire, the Governor is elected for only two years.

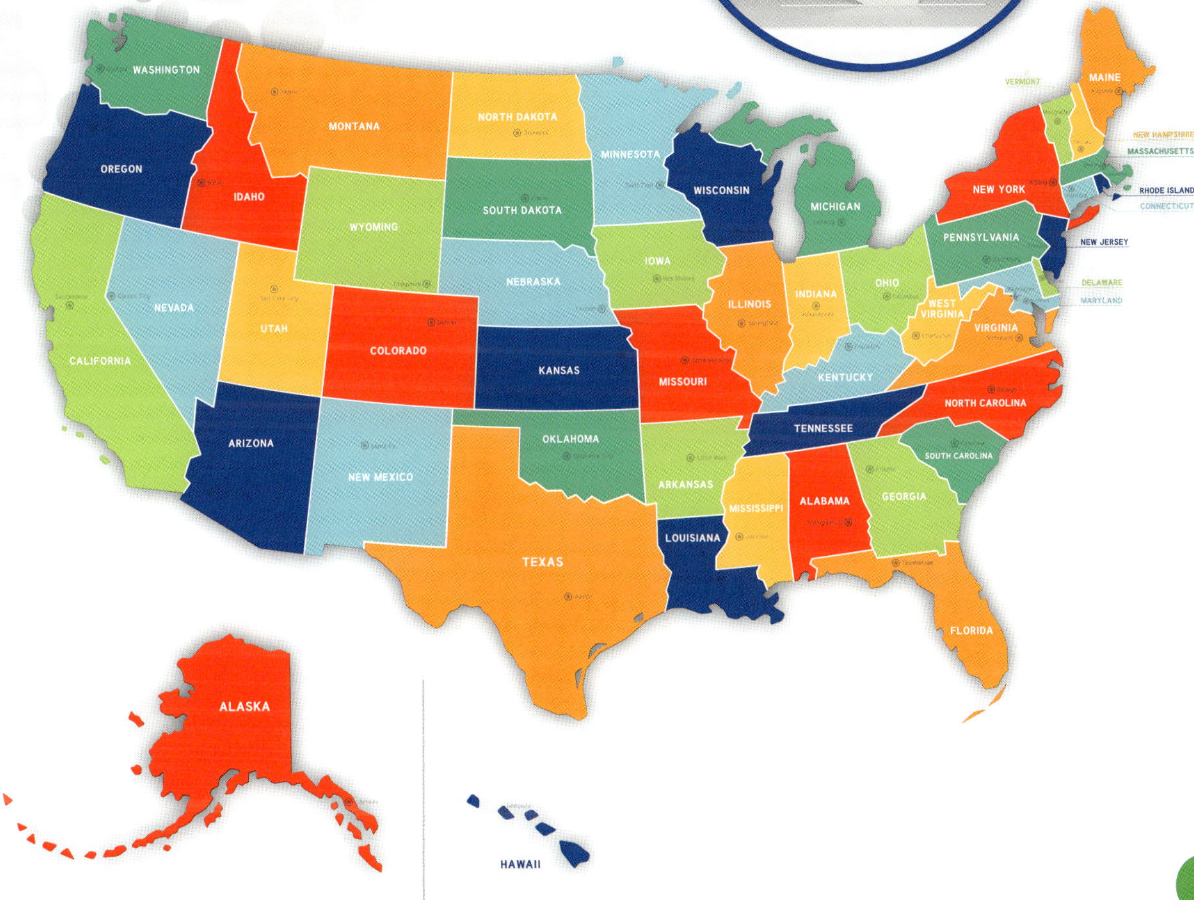

WASHINGTON
OREGON
CALIFORNIA
IDAHO
NEVADA
MONTANA
WYOMING
UTAH
ARIZONA
COLORADO
NEW MEXICO
NORTH DAKOTA
SOUTH DAKOTA
NEBRASKA
KANSAS
OKLAHOMA
TEXAS
MINNESOTA
IOWA
MISSOURI
ARKANSAS
LOUISIANA
WISCONSIN
ILLINOIS
MICHIGAN
INDIANA
OHIO
KENTUCKY
TENNESSEE
MISSISSIPPI
ALABAMA
GEORGIA
FLORIDA
SOUTH CAROLINA
NORTH CAROLINA
VIRGINIA
WEST VIRGINIA
PENNSYLVANIA
NEW YORK
VERMONT
MAINE
NEW HAMPSHIRE
MASSACHUSETTS
RHODE ISLAND
CONNECTICUT
NEW JERSEY
DELAWARE
MARYLAND
ALASKA
HAWAII

If the Governor wants to keep their job for another term, they must run for re-election.

In 36 states, the Governor is only allowed two terms in a row.

Many Governors and their families live in a special house.

It is called the Governor's Mansion.

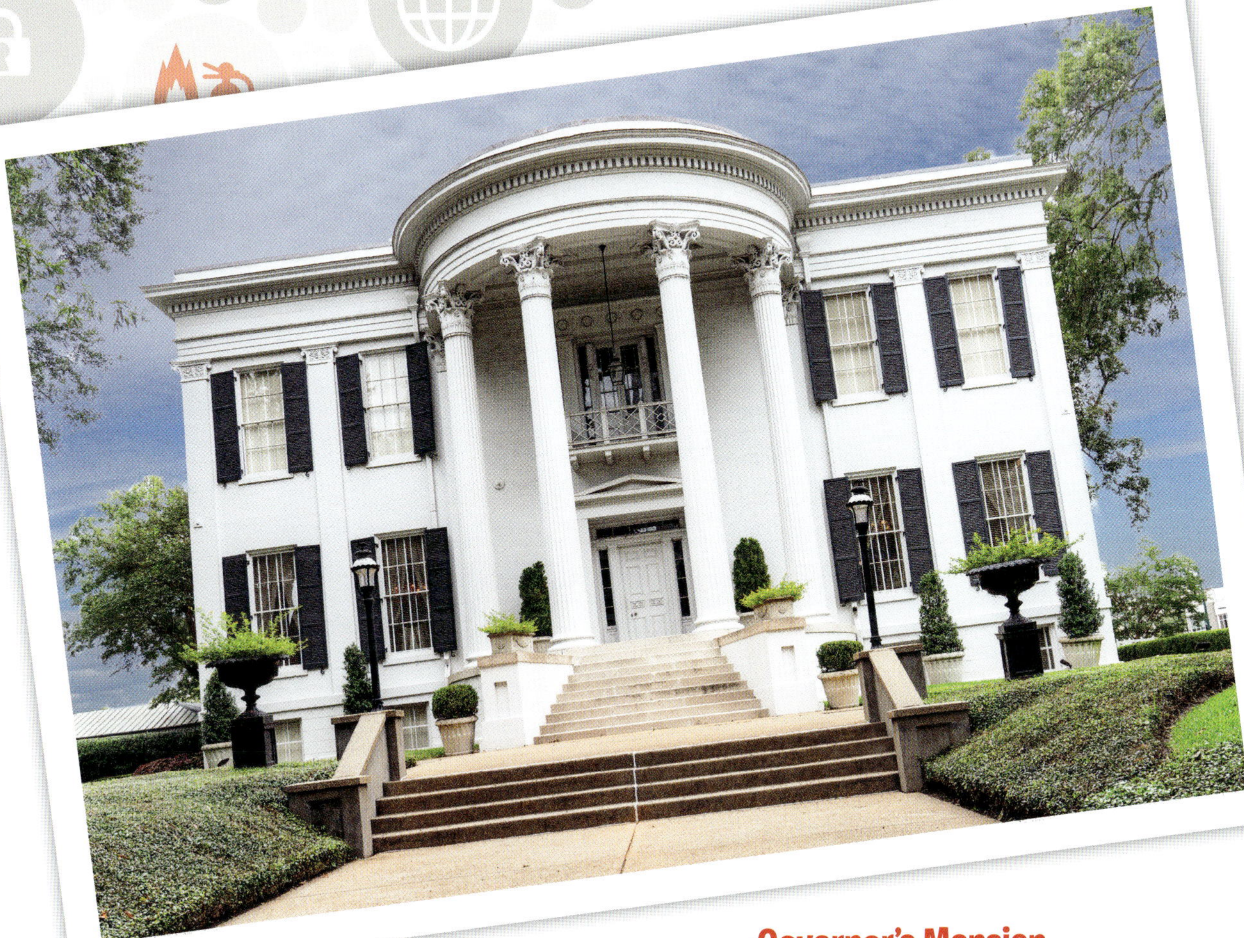

Governor's Mansion
Jackson, Mississippi

Governors approve laws written by lawmakers in their state.

They can also **veto** laws.

It is the Governor's job to **enforce** the laws of the state.

Governors choose people to work in state government. They choose judges.

They help decide how a state will spend its money.

Governors manage emergencies like floods and wildfires.

Each year, Governors tell the people how their state is doing.

This speech is called the State of the State Address.

NIA
REPUBLIC
SEAL OF THE GOVERNOR OF THE STATE OF CALIFORNIA
CALIFORNIA REPUBLIC
XL
NIA
REPUBLIC

President Bill Clinton was elected Governor of Arkansas in 1979 and again in 1983.

Nikki Haley was elected Governor of South Carolina in 2011.

President Bill Clinton
Governor of the state of Arkansas
1979 to 1981 and 1983 to 1992

Nikki Haley
Governor of the state of South Carolina
2011 to 2017

The Governor has an important job.

This leader makes sure that people are following state laws.

Words to Know

citizen (SIT-i-zuhn): a person who has the full rights of a country such as the right to live there, work there, and vote in its elections

enforce (en-FORS): to make sure that a law or rule is obeyed

government (GUHV-urn-muhnt): the system by which a country, state, or other organization is run; the group of people who govern

term (turm): a definite or limited period of time

veto (VEE-toh): the right of a President, Governor, or other top official to reject a bill that has been passed by lawmakers and to keep it from becoming a law

Index

Comprehension Questions

1. Who elects the Governor?
  a. lawmakers
  b. people across the United States
  c. people in the state

2. In most states, how long is the Governor's term?
  a. two years
  b. four years
  c. six years

3. **True or False:** A Governor is in charge of a state's government.

4. **True or False:** Governors are not allowed to decide how a state spends money.

5. **True or False:** Once a Governor's term is over, they can run for re-election.

Answers
1. c 2. b 3. True 4. False 5. True

About the Author

Stephanie Gaston is a journalist who has covered major stories including presidential inaugurations, natural disasters, and royal weddings. She has spent over a decade working in news for both local and major networks like CNN. Stephanie is a first-generation Haitian-American who grew up in Ft. Lauderdale, FL, a diverse community with Latin and Caribbean influences. In addition to being a writer, Stephanie is a dog lover, movie buff, fitness enthusiast, and most importantly, a proud mom.

Written by: Stephanie Gaston
Design by: Jen Bowers
Editor: Kim Thompson

Library of Congress PCN Data
Governor / Stephanie Gaston
The Job of a Civic Leader
ISBN 978-1-6389-7968-5 (hard cover)
ISBN 979-8-8873-5027-1 (paperback)
ISBN 979-8-8873-5086-8 (EPUB)
ISBN 979-8-8873-5145-2 (eBook)
Library of Congress Control Number: 2022942004

Printed in the United States of America.

Seahorse Publishing Company
www.seahorsepub.com

Copyright © 2023 **SEAHORSE PUBLISHING COMPANY**

All rights reserved. No part of this publication may be reproduced, stored in a retrieval system or be transmitted in any form or by any means, electronic, mechanical, photocopying, recording, or otherwise, without the prior written permission of Seahorse Publishing Company.

Published in the United States
Seahorse Publishing
PO Box 771325
Coral Springs, FL 33077

Photographs/Shutterstock: Cover and interior background circles © magic pictures, cover images ©2019 Terri Laurens, ©2018 Paul Brady Photography; p.3 legal pad ©2013 Mega Pixel, ©2021 Ron Adar, © Fourleaflover; p.4 ©2020 New Africa; p.5 ©2015 LifetimeStock; p.7 ©2016 AntonSokolov, © Fourleaflover; p.9 ©2021 Gorodenkoff; p.10 © Margarita Fedorenko; p.11 ©2019 Paul Brady Photography; p.12 ©2018 create jobs 51, © Aquir; p.13 ©2021 Emilia Dragomir; p.15 ©2021 Gorodenkoff, ©2017 Brian A Jackson, ©2018 24Novembers; p.17 ©2022 Sheila Fitzgerald; p.19 Public Domain/Official White House photo, Public Domain/United States Department of State; p.20 © Vladvm; p.21 ©2018 YP_Studio

SEAHORSE PUBLISHING